GOBBLE IT UP!

A RAFTER OF RECIPES
FOR
LEFTOVER TURKEY

(So Tasty You May
Want To Cook
Another Turkey!)

Joan LeGro Bushnell

For further information
or to order additional copies of this book
email: wordpainter1234@gmail.com

Printed in the United States of America

ISBN: 978-0-615-87933-8

A & C PUBLISHING
AC-Publishing.com

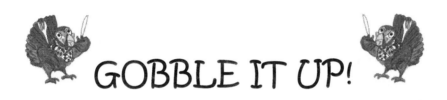

GOBBLE IT UP!

THE TURKEY IS A FUNNY BIRD,
ITS VERY NAME A FUNNY WORD,
ITS *RAISON D'ÊTRE* SHORT AND SWEET –
IT'S PRETTY BLOOMIN' GOOD TO EAT!

IT'S FOUND IN SANDWICHES AND STEW,
IT COMES IN SOUPS AND SALADS, TOO,
AND WHETHER CHILLED OR OVER HEAT,
IT'S PRETTY BLOOMIN' GOOD TO EAT!

IT MAKES A TASY DIET FARE
IN CASE YOU WANT TO TRY IT THERE;
FOR HOLIDAYS IT CAN'T BE BEAT –
IT'S PRETTY BLOOMIN' GOOD TO EAT!

SO, WHY NOT GIVE THIS BIRD A BREAK?
JUST TAKE THESE RECIPES AND MAKE
THE MOST OF THIS DELICIOUS MEAT –
IT'S PRETTY BLOOMIN' GOOD TO EAT!

--JLB

GOBBLE IT UP!

TABLE OF CONTENTS

...TABLE OF CONTENTS CONT.

OUT OF THE FRYING PAN INTO THE OVEN

LET'S TALK TURKEY

LET'S TALK TURKEY

Ah, yes, I *do* remember it, my first published recipe and, would you believe, it was for Leftover Turkey!

I was fresh out of college and jumping around from one job to another trying rather haphazardly to find whatever path it was I was meant to follow. One of those jobs was a volunteer position as editor of the small newspaper published by my sorority and this was how I found myself going to press early one November with a big need for a little filler.

The recipe was not exactly innovative, being practically a repeat of Thanksgiving dinner itself, but it did fill the need and fit the space. I was grateful then to dream it up and I am grateful now that it was so simple that I have no problem remembering it as follows.

LEFTOVER THANKSGIVING TURKEY: Lightly grease an oven-proof glass baking pan. Begin with a layer of sliced turkey and cover this with leftover gravy. Top it all with a layer of dressing and bake @ 350F for 35 minutes until gravy begins to bubble and dressing begins to crisp. Run under broiler for 5 minutes if needed.

The domestic turkey of today, as we know it, is descended from the wild turkey, the only breed of poultry native to the Western Hemisphere.

The wild turkey is believed to have originated in Mexico and fossil evidence shows proof of its dating back ten million years in the Americas. It was one of the earliest animals to be domesticated in these parts.

This bird continues to reside throughout North America. Due to overhunting and deforestation resulting in the destruction of its habitat, it became almost extinct during the 1930's but is once again found in all of the United States except Alaska.

The wild turkey still heads the list of most widely hunted birds. Despite the fact that it has no ears, it has excellent hearing and sight three times better than humans. With eyes on the sides of its head, a wild turkey has a 270-360 degree field of vision and can see in color. It can detect motion up to 100 yards away giving it a real advantage in eluding its hunters, thus the well-earned title of most popular game bird.

Although its night vision is poor, this bird compensates by residing in trees in grassy areas. It favors the oak tree and will fly up to roost at sunset then come down at first light to feed on seeds and, sometimes, insects in the grass below.

A wild turkey can run at speeds up to 25 mph and, in a matter of seconds, with a wing span of 4.5 feet, burst into flight for a short period of time at speeds of 50-55mph then glide as far as a mile without flapping its wings.

Christopher Columbus is said to have discovered and named the North American turkey during his travels to the New World where it had long been a staple in the diets of Native American tribes, and the bird began to appear in Spain and Britain sometime during the 1500's. Thinking the land he had discovered was connected to India, Columbus called this bird *tuka*, the word for "peacock" in Tamil, an Indian language. (The fact that the turkey is a type of pheasant seems to have little to do with his theory.)

Another premise suggests that the bird's name comes from its Native American name, *firkee.* For all we know, it could be a combination of both. That is, unless you're willing to believe as some do, that the turkey's name is derived from the "turk, turk, turk" sound this bird makes when frightened.

Can't you just see some poor, terrified turkey running from a bunch of hungry settlers at the dizzying speed of 25 mph while trying to give its name, rank and serial number in hope of a pardon?

The pardon was a long time in coming.

For centuries before, Native Americans and First Nations had been celebrating and giving thanks for their harvests just as English and European farmers celebrated this seasonable abundance of good food with a cornucopia or horn of plenty, a curved goat's horn filled with fruits and grain.

The first Thanksgiving celebration in North America is acknowledged by many to have taken place in Canada when English explorer Martin Frobisher and his crew arrived in Newfoundland in 1578 wanting to give thanks for their safe arrival in the New World.

Although the first American Thanksgiving, as we know it, is traced to Plymouth in present-day Massachusetts, this harvest festival did not become an annual affair in New England until the late 1660's. There is ongoing debate as to the exact location of the first American Thanksgiving by the descendants of Florida, Texas and Virginia colonists who continue to contend that *their* forefathers were the first to set foot on what was to become American soil.

President George Washington proclaimed the first nation-wide American Thanksgiving November 26, 1789 but it was not celebrated annually until 1863 when President Abraham Lincoln set aside the last Thursday in November "as a day for national thanksgiving and prayer."

In 1879 Canada declared "a day of general Thanksgiving to Almighty God for the bountiful harvest with which Canada has been blessed." This day was celebrated annually on November 6th until 1957 when it was changed to the second Monday in October to correspond more closely with harvest time and to avoid conflict with Remembrance (Armistice) Day on November 11th.

As for that presidential pardon, it's thought by some that the first one dates back to the day in 1863 when Abraham Lincoln took pity on his son Tad's pet turkey. However, it seems a more likely possibility, as is thought by others, that President Harry Truman pardoned the turkey given to him in 1947 by The *National Turkey Federation* and the *Poultry and Egg National Board*, beginning a tradition which continues to this day.

Accordingly, President John F. Kennedy is quoted as having said, "Let's just keep him," in 1963 and President George H.W. Bush officially pardoned his Thanksgiving oblation for the first time in 1989.

While granting his presidential pardon at Thanksgiving time, 2012, Barak Obama made note of the fact that the turkey, like anyone else, should have "a second chance," no doubt referring to his own reelection earlier that month.

Domestic turkeys are bred for breast meat and so heavy that they cannot get off the ground. They are also bred to have white feathers which leave no spots under the skin after plucking.

Most turkeys raised for commercial use are White Hollands.

Male turkeys are called *toms.* Females are called *hens.* Juvenile toms are *jakes* and juvenile females are *jennies.*

A hen can lay about 115 eggs per month and these eggs take 28 days to hatch.

Baby turkeys are called *poults*. A University of Arkansas study states that turkey poults require four 2-hour periods of rest per day in addition to 8-10 hours of nighttime sleep and are trained to eat several small meals per day in order to avoid gorging themselves. (This sounds pretty good to me!)

A 16 week-old turkey is called a *fryer* and a male turkey can grow to 20 pounds within 18 weeks after hatching. A 5-7 month-old is called a *young roaster;* a year-old turkey is a *yearling.* Any turkey fifteen months or older is called *mature.*

Contrary to what one might think, older larger male turkeys are more tender and flavorful than younger birds or females. Google's Turkey Trivia tells us that old hens can be tough birds. Where have we heard this before?

Turkey is a wonder food.

In addition to being delicious, turkey is nutritious. It's low in calories, cholesterol, fat and sodium and high in protein and rich in vitamins, particularly B-12 and selenium. Google lists turkey as one of the top ten foods for healthy eyesight as it is rich in zinc and niacin to protect against cataracts. It has about 70% white meat with fewer calories and less fat than dark while the greater flavor in dark meat is perfect for soups and stews or grilling and barbecue.

Because I have to assume you will know how to cook a turkey in order to find yourself with its leftovers, I have left out the conventional means of preparation in order to make room for some of the more unusual ones. I have, however, included a few pieces of information I could have used myself on that first Thanksgiving when the responsibility fell to me. This was the year I learned a lot about cooking between Thanksgiving and Christmas!

And, that's all she wrote back in those days but she has learned a few tricks since then and, hopefully, you will find the recipes herein considerably more interesting and helpful.

This little book brings to the table a rafter of recipes for turkey lovers.

My WEBSTER ENCYCLOPEDIC UNABRIDGED DICTIONARY defines *rafter* as *a flock, esp. of turkeys* so, with just a soupçon of poetic license, here we are with a flock of recipes for turkey lovers.

Recently, after a long night of pondering the seemingly limitless possibilities leftover turkey has to offer, I may have been hallucinating when the *eft* in *leftover* suddenly disappeared leaving me with *lover*. Nevertheless, in my diminished capacity I wondered drowsily if this could be some kind of sign. Indeed, it was! My alter ego (WEBSTER'S EUD) defines the word *eft* as *1. again 2. afterward.* "Leftover" is "lover again or afterward."

Surely this was meant to be, this little book of turkey leftovers for turkey lovers.

Turkey is easy and fun to cook and easy and fun to eat and It isn't just for holiday time. It's economical, too. When you consider the number of meals you can get from a turkey and the endless variety of things you can do with this wonder food, it's no wonder you'll want to purchase extra and

GOBBLE IT UP!!!

Canada is one of the world's largest producers of turkey ranking sixth out of ten. Turkeys are raised year round in special barns and their feathers are spread out on fields and plowed under in spring. The feathers decompose and fertilize the soil. Canadian consumption of turkey meat has remained relatively stable over the past two decades at 2.2 pounds per person per year.

While dark meat is preferred in most countries, white meat is the favorite in the United States.

Americans consume 18 pounds of turkey per capita every year. Its mild flavor lends itself to ethnic dishes as a substitute for high fat meats. Fifty percent of American consumers eat turkey at least once a week and nearly 88% surveyed by the National Turkey Federation eat turkey at Thanksgiving.

North Carolina produces more turkey than any other state annually. Minnesota is second and Arkansas is third.

The top turkey-eating nation is Israel whose citizens consume about 28 pounds per person annually.

TURKEY TIPS

Should you not happen to have the real thing on hand nor the need to cook the *whole* thing and feel you simply must have one of these wonderful recipes, you will find that cooked ground turkey may be substituted for many. Therefore, I am including it here. Don't forget, though, that a small 10-12 turkey is easy to cook and a whole lot more bang for your buck!

BUYING TURKEY:

5-7 month "Toms" are thought to be most tender.

Allow ½- ¾ lb *per serving* not per person,
    ¾-1 lb *per person.*

2 c ground turkey = about 1 lb

STORING TURKEY:

Refrigerator: Fresh turkey – 2 days
                  Ground turkey – 1 day
                  Cooked turkey – up to 4 days
                  Gravy and stuffing – 1 to 2 days

Freezer: Fresh turkey – 2-3 months
             Ground turkey – 2-3 months
             Cooked turkey – up to 4 months
             Gravy and stuffing – about 1 month

NEVER store turkey above 40F (4C).

Commercially frozen pre-stuffed turkeys should not be thawed before cooking.

NEVER refreeze a thawed turkey.

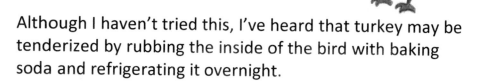

PREPARING TURKEY:

Although I haven't tried this, I've heard that turkey may be tenderized by rubbing the inside of the bird with baking soda and refrigerating it overnight.

COOKING TURKEY:

Fresh turkeys may cook somewhat faster than those which have been frozen.

Stuffed turkeys take longer to cook than unstuffed ones.

NEVER roast a turkey at temperature low enough for bacteria to form.

As a rule of thumb, in a low to moderate oven (300-325F or 150-165C), allow about 25 minutes per pound for birds under 12 pounds and 20 minutes per pound for larger birds.

Breasts and thighs take 1 to 1¾ hours to cook.

A meat thermometer in the thickest part of the thigh and away from the bone should register 175-180F (80-82C).

Whole turkey is done when legs wriggle easily and thigh juices run clear when pierced.

If turkey gets too brown, cover it loosely with foil for the last third of cooking time.

CARVING TURKEY:

After removing from oven, let the bird rest, loosely covered, for about 15 minutes.
Remove drumsticks and thighs.
Holding the turkey with a large fork, carve inward toward breast bone.

There are numerous other means by which to cook whole turkey. Here are a few choices. Have a good flight!

ROTISSERIE TURKEY

TURKEY ON A SPIT

SMOKED BEER CAN TURKEY
See About.com for "About Barbecues & Grilling"

COOKING A TURKEY OVER A CAMPFIRE

COOKING A TURKEY UNDERGROUND

GARBAGE CAN TURKEY
Said to cook in 90 minutes!
 See YouTube.ca

COOKING A TURKEY IN A PAPER BAG
This method is not recommended as the cooking temperature is so low that bacteria may be present.

BARBECUED TURKEY OVER CHARCOAL WITH PEPPERED PEACH GLAZE

Place aluminum foil drip pan in center of covered grill then add 8-12 charcoal briquettes on each side to prepare medium fire (when coals turn white).

Meanwhile, remove giblets from 10-12 pound turkey (reserve for gravy or soup).

Rinse turkey and pat dry inside and out with paper towel. Season with salt and pepper and other seasonings as desired.

Stuff cavity with 1 onion and 1 apple, cut in half if needed. It's not necessary to peel or core these; wash apple and remove outer skin from onion.

Optional: Add 4 lemon quarters dusted with ⅛ c or 2 T dried sage.

Insert thermometer in meatiest part of thigh (away from bone).

When coals begin to turn white, oil grill rack and set over fire.

You may place bird breast side down on rack over drip pan and grill, covered, for 20 min before turning it breast side up but I don't find this necessary.

Grill turkey, covered, breast side up until temperature reaches 170-180F (75-80C).

These temperatures should also apply to turkey barbecued on gas or electric grills.

Cook time should total about 2½ hrs or until leg wriggles easily, juices run clear and meat is white to the bone. Remove bird from fire, tent with foil and let rest 15-30 min before carving.

Optional: For **PEPPERED PEACH GLAZE** heat together 1 c peach preserves, ½ c white wine, 1 T oil, ¾ t fresh-ground pepper & 2 T chopped fresh ginger or 1 t dried ginger until preserves melt (about 5 min). Brush bird 2 or 3 times during last ½ hr before finish time.

VERTICALLY ROASTED TURKEY

There is a variety of vertical roasters on the market, the advantage to this method being a shorter cooking time with the finished product much lower in fat than that of any other method. "Stand-up roasting," as our daughter used to call it, makes for a tender, juicier bird with extra crisp skin. Remove all but bottom rack and preheat oven to 400F (200C).
Coat vertical roaster with nonstick cooking spray and place on large shallow roasting pan.
Remove giblets from 10-12 lb turkey. Reserve these for gravy or soup.
Rinse inside and out and pat dry with paper towel.
Season inside cavity and outside skin with your favorite seasoning or simply salt and pepper, if desired.
To fit turkey into oven, cut off the tail then stand bird on roaster. Push down and seat firmly so that the top of the roaster comes through the neck cavity then clip excess neck bone even with top of roaster. Put this into stock pot with giblets.
Add 1" water, wine, beer or juice to pan and place on bottom oven rack.

"Blast" the bird @ 400F (200C) for 30 min
then reduce heat to 350F (175C) and
continue to cook for 12-15 min per lb
adding 5 min per lb for every 1000 (305m)
feet above sea level or until thermometer
inserted in meatiest part of thigh reaches
180F (80C).
For browner, crispier skin raise, oven
temperature to 450F (230C) for 5-10 minutes at end of
cooking.
Keep in mind that oven temperatures can vary
and cooking times may need to be adjusted.
Use some of liquid in pan for gravy.

STUFFING

To stuff bird, plan on ¾ stuffing per pound of turkey.
BUT REMEMBER - an unstuffed turkey will take less time (1-3 min per lb) to cook and you can make a lot more stuffing in a large casserole than in a turkey cavity.
Stuffing will have the same good flavor if baked in a casserole and basted with drippings from the turkey pan.

STOCK FOR GRAVY

Canned chicken broth may be substituted for stock but homemade stock, easy enough to make, is much better.
To make stock combine giblets with a couple of celery stalks with leaves, a couple of carrots, an onion cut up, a small bunch of parsley, a couple of chicken bouillon cubes, your seasonings of choice, and water to cover. Simmer for an hour or two while turkey cooks, adding water as necessary.

GRAVY

You may transfer turkey from roasting pan to platter and make gravy in pan.
Pour off excess fat and scrape pan to get as much "brown" as possible.
Blend ¼ c flour with ¼ c fat and juice from roasting pan.
Place 6 c stock in large pot and gradually mix in flour mixture till smooth.
Bring to boil and cook, stirring, until thickened. Thin with additional stock or broth as necessary and add milk or half and half as desired.
If needed, enrich color with bottled gravy browner.

COUSIN ADDIE'S BREAD DRESSING

(Another handwritten special from my mother's collection.)*

1 lg loaf of bread, broken small
About ¼ lb butter
2 tsp salt
2 med sized onions

Cook celery and onions in butter – do not brown. Add bread and mix.

*I have to commend Cousin Addie for her simplicity. She leaves us with a true sense of the basics. However, I must confess here that I like to add at least a pinch of sage and a couple of cups of chopped celery.

MY MOTHER'S BARBECUE SAUCE

(This, too, from my mother's book of "Cooking Clips" although I have no recollection of ever having seen her anywhere near a barbecue!)

½ c salad oil
1 t paprika
1½ c water
1 t pepper
2 T chopped onion
½ t dry mustard
1 clove garlic, crushed
1½ t sugar
2 T vinegar
1 t salt
1 t chili powder
1 t Worcestershire sauce
1 t Tabasco
Dash cayenne

Combine all ingredients & simmer about 30 minutes to blend flavors.

...................TURKEY FACTS.......................

Mother Nature Network tells us that, contrary to widespread belief, Benjamin Franklin (1706-1790) did not actually suggest that the wild turkey represent his country. His official recommendation for America's symbol was, in fact, an image of Moses and Pharaoh.

After the bald eagle was chosen for this honor the scientist turned statesman complained in a letter to his daughter that this bird was a cowardly scavenger while the turkey was a "much more respectable bird."

* *

President Andrew Jackson (1767-1845) maintained that his #1 favorite food was turkey hash!

The first mission to orbit the moon arrived on Christmas Eve 1968. According to historian Andrew Chaikin, "In Apollo 8's food locker, wrapped in foil and tied with red and green ribbons: real turkey with stuffing and cranberry sauce."
American astronauts Frank Borman, James Lovell and Bill Anders described their holiday surprise as "by far the best meal of the voyage."

A few months later on their Apollo 11 mission in July 1969, the first two humans to set foot on the moon, American astronauts Neil Armstrong and Edwin Eugene "Buzz" Aldrin along with their command module pilot Michael Collins, ate turkey with all the trimmings in foil packages for their first meal on the moon.

STARTERS
SOUPS
SALADS
SANDWICHES
& SUCH

HORS D'OEUVRES BITES

See **BL-DOUBLE-T BITES.**
Omit lettuce. Cut sandwiches into 1" slices & secure with toothpicks.

MINI MEATBALLS

See **MY SWEDISH MEATBALLS.***
Form mixture into 3 dozen meatballs. Brown on all sides in butter or oil in skillet. Bake on cookie sheet for about 20 min @ 350 F (180 C).
Serve heated in sauce of 1 c catsup & 1 c classic yellow mustard.
*May be frozen on a cookie sheet & stored in freezer.

DEVILED TURKEY SPREAD

1 c minced cooked turkey
1 3-oz pkg cream cheese softened with 1 T cream
1 T each minced onion & celery
1 t curry powder

Combine these ingredients to form a soft paste.
Refrigerate 2 hrs.
Serve with assorted crackers.

JACK & TOMS

3 doz bite-size pieces cooked turkey
3 doz ½" squares Jack cheese
3 avocados
Juice of 2 lemons
½ c mayonnaise
½ c bottled honey mustard dressing

To do ahead:
Cut avocados into small pieces, sprinkle with lemon juice &
refrigerate.
"Spear" 1 each turkey piece & cheese square on toothpick.
Refrigerate.
Prepare mixture of mayonnaise & honey mustard for
dipping.

To serve:
Add avocado pieces to turkey & cheese. Arrange around
dipping sauce.

BL-DOUBLE-T BITES

(A variation of the BL-Double-T Sandwich, this takes a bit of time & patience but your guests will reach for more, so be sure to make plenty!)

16 slices bread of your choice
16 slices bacon, cooked crisp & crumbled finely
  1 c turkey paste (chopped turkey and about 4 T
        mayonnaise -- do this in small food processor)
3 doz cherry tomatoes, cut in half
 Shredded lettuce

Flatten bread with rolling pin or wine bottle.
Cut 4 circles from each slice with small round cookie cutter or liqueur glass. (See? You're on your way to the party already!)
Coat cookie sheet with non-stick spray & carefully toast bread rounds. It's best to do this on low, 250F (120C).
Combine bacon with turkey-mayonnaise mixture.
(This is a good do-ahead place to stop lest the lettuce get soggy.)

Just before serving, add small amount of lettuce to bacon/turkey/mayonnaise mixture. (You may have to chop even shredded lettuce somewhat to get it to fit on toast rounds.)
Spoon this onto toast rounds.
Top with cherry tomato.
Makes about 5 dozen

TURKEY MOUSSE

1 can condensed cream of chicken soup
1 pkg unflavored gelatin
1 8-oz pkg cream cheese @ room temperature
1 c finely chopped celery
4 finely chopped green onions
1 c mayonnaise
1 c finely chopped turkey

Heat soup, undiluted, and soften gelatin in it.
Add cream cheese and mix well.
Add celery & green onion then mayonnaise & turkey.
Turn into a 4-cup mold coated with nonstick spray.
Refrigerate for 8 hrs or overnight.
Unmold on greens.
Serve with crackers.

MY TURKEY SOUP

(We consider the base for this to be "stock" or "broth" and use it in a rafter of recipes!)

In large soup pot cover turkey carcass with cold water.
Depending upon size of carcass and amount of water, add 2-4 lg bouillon cubes, 1 lg onion peeled & cut into quarters, 2 lg carrots, cut into sections, 3 stalks celery & a bunch of parsley (or more).
Bring to boil, reduce heat and simmer, uncovered, about 3 hrs, adding water as necessary.
Remove from heat then pour through colander to remove bones.
Discard bones, skin, onion & celery.
Allow liquid to cool then refrigerate to let cool further.
Skim off fat.

Add to broth: 1 lg sweet onion, finely chopped
2-3 stalks celery, chopped
4 each med zucchini & yellow crook-neck squash, unpeeled, cut into chunks
1 pkg baby spinach (or 1-2 pkgs froz chopped spinach) or 1 pkg froz lima beans, cooked
Kernels from 2 lg ears corn (or 2 c froz)
Cook until vegetables are done.*
Add ½ pkg fine egg noodles, cooked.

*(You can always do this the traditional way with onions & carrots & potatoes.)

CREAM OF TURKEY-CABBAGE SOUP

(This is a satisfying supper for a cold winter night. Serve with cheese-sprinkled sour dough toast and Corn Relish Salad.)

1 head cabbage, cored & shredded*
1 lg carrot, grated*
1 lg onion, minced
6 c turkey broth (See **MY TURKEY SOUP**)*
1 c cream sauce*
3 c leftover turkey, cubed or in bite-size pieces

Combine cabbage, carrot & onion in soup pot with broth.
Bring to boil, reduce heat & simmer, uncovered, for 30 min.
Blend cream sauce into broth & add turkey.
Simmer about 10 min more.
Serve 6-8.

*If you're not a purist, you may want to do this "my way, the easy way" by substituting a pkg of cole slaw mix for the cabbage & carrot and canned broth or bouillon with condensed cream of chicken soup for the turkey soup base & cream sauce.

CORN RELISH SALAD: Your choice of greens tossed with our corn relish as follows. **VI'S DRESSING**: In a jar with tight-fitting lid, shake until smooth 1 c honey, ¾ c cider vinegar, ½ c olive oil & 1 T celery seed. Store in refrigerator. **CORN RELISH**: Combine dressing as needed with 2 cans kernel corn, drained, or 2½ c cooked fresh corn. Add about ½ c minced celery, ½ c minced green onions with greens & 2 T finely chopped pimiento. Toss with mixed greens.

TURKEY SENEGALESE SOUP
(This is traditionally served chilled but may be served hot.)

Mix together: 1 can condensed cream of chicken soup
               1 can chicken bouillon
               1 c heavy cream
               1 pkg Hollandaise Sauce Mix (dry)
               1 t curry powder
               Salt & fresh ground pepper to taste
               1 c minced cooked turkey
               Juice of 1 lemon
               4 T finely chopped apple

Combine first 6 ingredients.
Stir in turkey and squeeze in lemon juice.
Spoon into soup cups, chill or heat well, sprinkle apple on top and serve. Serves 4

MARY'S TURKEY GRAPE SALAD
(This is a wonderful summertime buffet or luncheon dish!)

4 c cooked turkey, cut into bite-size pieces
2 c each green & red grapes, cut in half
1 small (4 oz) pkg cream cheese @ room temperature
1 c mayonnaise
1 c sour cream
1 c unsalted walnut pieces

Mix mayonnaise & sour cream and mash in cream cheese. Fold in turkey & grapes. Cover and refrigerate for 4 hrs. Add walnuts and serve on platter or individual plates over variegated lettuce with mini croissants and something icy for dessert.
Serves 8

BARBARA'S CHILLED TURKEY LOAF
(A do-ahead special for a special lunch!)

1 T unflavored gelatin
¼ c cold water
2 T fresh lemon juice
1¾ c turkey stock or chicken broth
1½ c finely chopped turkey*
1 c mayonnaise
½ c finely chopped raw celery*
Salt to taste
1 hard cooked egg, sliced
4-6 sliced ripe olives
1 pkg shredded lettuce or 1 pkg baby spinach
Bottled Vinaigrette

Let gelatin stand in cold water 5 min while bringing ¼ c stock to boil.

Stir boiling stock into gelatin then stir until mixture is dissolved.

Stir in 1½ c cold turkey stock with lemon juice.

Cover & refrigerate until set (about as thick as cold raw egg whites).

Meanwhile, coat a 4-cup mold or 6 individual molds *lightly* with non-stick cooking spray.

To add garnish, place egg and/or olive slices in small amount of gelatin mix (about ¼") in bottom of mold(s) and refrigerate.

When garnish is set (about 1 hr), stir turkey, celery & ½ c mayonnaise into gelatin mixture, pour this into mold or individual molds** and cover with plastic wrap.
Refrigerate 8 hrs or overnight.
Unmold on shredded lettuce or bed of baby spinach.
Drizzle greens lightly with vinaigrette and serve with remainder of mayonnaise.
Serves 6

*I like to "chop" turkey and celery in my blender with some of the stock then strain and proceed.

** If you have a small ring mold, you may want to serve extra mayonnaise in center. Just for fun, you may even want to add a couple of drops of food coloring to mayonnaise.

TURKEY SOUR CREAM ASPIC

(From my mother's "Cooking Clips." Origin unknown.)

3½ c diced turkey
2 envelopes unflavored gelatin
¼ c cold water
1 t onion juice
3 T lemon juice
1 t dry mustard
2 c hot turkey stock or chicken broth
1½ c sour cream
1 c chopped celery
½ c chopped roasted almonds
1½ t curry (Optional)

Soak gelatin in cold water. Add onion juice, lemon juice & mustard to hot stock – then gelatin mixture -- & stir until dissolved. Let cool & mix sour cream in well. Let cool in refrigerator until starting to thicken (about 1 hr) then add turkey, celery & nuts. Refrigerate until firm, 8 hrs or overnight. May be made in individual moulds or one large one.
Serves about 8

TURCADO WRAP

1 c minced turkey
1 T each minced celery & onion
1 sm tomato, peeled* & chopped
1 ripe avocado
1 T mayonnaise
1 T sour cream
1 t Worcestershire
Pinch gr cumin
Seasoning to taste
4-8 lg lettuce leaves
4 lg flour tortillas

Mix together first 3 ingredients then mash in avocado.
Mix in next 4 ingredients (mayonnaise & sour cream as
    needed).
Season to taste.
Wrap in lettuce then tortillas... unless you want to skip
    tortillas for a lo-cal snack!
Serves 4.

*To remove skin, submerge tomato in boiling water for
about 30 seconds.

MY FAVORITE SANDWICH

Spread 2 slices pumpernickel, rye or marble bread liberally
with 1000 ISLAND DRESSING* and layer as follows:

> Sliced turkey
> Sliced Swiss cheese
> Thinly-sliced tomato
> Sliced hard-cooked egg

*1000 ISLAND DRESSING: 1 T mayonnaise
                        1T sour cream
                        1 T catsup

MY OTHER FAVORITE SANDWICH

Split whole wheat Kaiser rolls and spread both sides liberally with bottled Honey Mustard.

Layer bottom half with: sliced turkey
sliced provolone
shredded lettuce
chopped ripe olive

Replace top, cut into sections and serve.

BL-DOUBLE-T SANDWICH

Your favorite bread (I like this on a lightly-toasted Kaiser roll)

Tomato slices
Shredded lettuce
Cooked turkey, thinly sliced
Crisp-cooked bacon, finely chopped
Mayonnaise

Combine bacon with mayonnaise to make paste.
Spread both sides of bread (toast) liberally.
Build sandwich with lettuce, turkey & tomato. *(This can easily be converted to hors d'oeuvres.)*

*HORS D'OEUVRES BITES: Reduce or omit lettuce, cut sandwiches into 1" slices & secure with toothpicks.

TURKEY REUBEN

Per sandwich: 2 slices rye or pumpernickel bread
             2 slices Swiss cheese
             See 1000 Island Dressing (MY FAVORITE SANDWICH)
             2-4 slices cooked turkey breast
             Sauerkraut

Spread both slices of bread liberally with dressing.
On first slice, build upward with 1 slice cheese, turkey & sauerkraut, and second slice cheese.
Spread outside of bread lightly but evenly with butter.
Place in pan over med heat and weigh down with another pan.
Cook, turning, until cheese is melted and bread is toasted.

TURKEY LUNCH KA-BOBS
(Kids will love these lunchbox surprises!)

Alternate on wooden skewers: turkey chunks
                                    pineapple chunks
                                    cherry tomatoes
                                    cheese cubes

Other choices may include: olives
                                    pickles
                                    grapes
                                    carrot slices
                                    cucumber slices
                                    zucchini slices
                                    Bell pepper pieces
                                    celery bits

You can purchase small pkgs of dressing for dipping or make
up your own.
Use your imagination and cater to your child's preferences.
Cradle in ice-filled sealable plastic bags for travel.

CURRIED TURKEY AND EGGS

(Found in an old handwritten recipe file of "Cooking Clips" belonging to my mother. Origin unknown.)

¼ c butter
¼ c minced green pepper
2 T minced onion
¼ c flour
2½ c milk
1 T lemon juice
1 t curry powder
Salt & pepper to taste
1½ c diced, cooked turkey
¾ c cooked peas
3 hard-cooked eggs, sliced
6 slices bread
6 slices cheese

Melt butter in skillet; add green pepper & onion; cook until soft; stir in flour then milk; cook, stirring until thick.
Blend in lemon juice, curry powder, salt & pepper.
Stir in turkey, peas & eggs.
Trim crusts from bread slices.*
Toast on one side then turn and top each with slice of cheese. Broil until brown and cut into quarters.
Spoon turkey mixture into serving dish; top with cheese triangles; bake @ 350F (175C) 30 min.
Serves 6

*Freeze crusts for stuffing or bread crumbs.

MY PLAIN OL' TURKEY PIE

(If you want to have some fun some rainy Saturday morning, try putting this together with one of your youngest.)

1 frozen deep dish pie shell (They come in pkgs of 2 and you'll need the 2nd one for your topping.)
2 c cooked turkey meat in bite-size pieces
1-2 pkgs frozen mixed vegetables
1 can condensed cream of chicken soup
1-2 T heavy cream
1 c cooked rice (Minute Rice is good)
Turkey-shape cookie cutter or other shape suitable for the occasion.

Follow pkg directions for baking crust and proceed.
Mix turkey, vegetables, rice, soup & cream.
Season to your liking and turn into pie crust.
Now, for the fun.
If you're lucky enough to be artistically inclined, you may want to cut out your own turkey from extra crust. If not, any bird-shaped cutter will work (like those little chickies & duckies we use at Easter).* Just place a rafter of them on top of your pie and, there, you have it!

*You may have to bake your little birdies separately on a cookie sheet if your bottom crust has been baked first.

TURKEY FACTS

Turkeys give us more than a diverse menu.

Turkey skins are tanned to make belts, cowboy boots and other accessories.

Turkey down makes pillows.

Turkey feathers make Native American costumes and quills for pens.

Spurs of wild toms were once used by Native Americans as projectiles on arrowheads.

...............TURKEY FACTS...........................

A turkey has 157 bones.

Native Americans hunted wild turkey for its meat as early as 1000 A.D. and made "callers" from the wing bones. Hundreds of years later wild turkey became a source of food for early settlers.

Turkey callers are still used to call turkeys to the hunt.

OUT OF THE FRYING PAN INTO THE OVEN

SLOPPY TOMS

(If you like Sloppy Joes you'll love this lo-cal, lo-chol quick and healthy alternative for those on the go. For added convenience keep chopped onion and pepper, prepared ahead or bought commercially, in your freezer. If you have all ingredients handy, you can put this together in 10 minutes!)

3 c cooked turkey, chopped
1 c each onion & yellow Bell pepper, chopped
½ c catsup
½ c classic yellow mustard
2 T Worcestershire
2 T olive oil
4 hamburger buns or Kaiser rolls

Sauté onion and pepper in olive oil over med heat until softened.
Add turkey and stir in catsup, mustard and Worcestershire until well blended.
Continue stirring until hot enough to serve.
Serve piping hot over toasted rolls with extra sauce for dipping.
Serves 4

QUICK SKILLET SUPPER

6 slices bacon in 1" pieces
1 sweet onion, thinly sliced
1 c uncooked small elbow macaroni
2½ c water
1 can condensed cream of chicken soup
3 c cooked turkey, diced
1 c grated Parmesan or Swiss cheese

In lg skillet with cover, brown bacon. Remove from pan &
drain on paper towels.
Sauté onion in bacon fat until golden. Drain onion & remove
any excess fat from pan.
Mix soup with water. Place with macaroni in pan.
Bring to boil, cover, & cook until macaroni is done, about 10
min.
Add turkey, mix well & heat about 5 min.
Fold in cheese until melted.
Serve sprinkled with bacon pieces.
Serves 6

TURKEY-STUFFED PEPPER WITH TOMATO SAUCE

(These freeze well and I like to put together a couple of extra batches for the freezer when Bell peppers and corn are in season)

4 lg green Bell Pepper, cut in half, seeds removed
2 c cooked turkey, chopped
1 carrot & ½ c onion, chopped and sautéed in 2 T olive oil
Kernels from 1 ear corn (about 1 c)
1 c cooked brown rice
Sm can tomato paste (reserve ½ for sauce)
½ c chicken broth
1 T Worcestershire Sauce
1 c Parmesan cheese, grated
Salt & pepper to taste

Mix just enough chicken broth with tomato paste to hold stuffing mixture together. Reserve the rest for sauce.
Combine remaining ingredients and stuff pepper halves.
Sprinkle with cheese.
Place on cookie sheet or shallow roasting pan with just enough water to cover bottom.
Spoon sauce over and bake @300F (150C) for 1 hour.

SAUCE:

Remainder of tomato paste
Remainder of chicken broth
1 small can sliced ripe olives
Dash Tabasco (optional)

Heat these ingredients together in small saucepan. Thicken with 1t cornstarch if necessary. Pour over peppers.
Serves 6-8

DANNY'S TURKEY-CABBAGE-TOMATO BAKE

(She made mine so much better that I had to put her name on it! She calls it "comfort food for a cold winter's night.")

2 Big cans Chicken Broth or Better than Bouillon
1 Small head cabbage – shredded
2 Leeks, sliced – white part only*
5 Small redskin potatoes, diced
1½ c cooked turkey, cut into bites – about ¾" sq
Generous sprinkle of paprika,
Salt & generous freshly cracked pepper
Lots of dill weed – about 1 T
1 regular can peeled, crushed tomatoes, undrained
8 oz sour cream
About ½ c bread crumbs
About ½ c shredded Parmesan
Butter

1) In lg pot bring chicken broth to boil, add cabbage, potatoes & leeks, bring back to boil for 5 minutes.
2) Drain well & cool to room temp.
3) In large mixing bowl layer veggies/turkey/tomatoes/sour cream & sprinkle with seasonings. Stir gently to combine.
4) Fold into buttered casserole.
Can make ahead to this point & refrigerate overnight.
5) Top with bread crumbs & shredded Parmesan. Dot with butter.
6) Bake 350F (180C) – 30-40 minutes 'til slightly bubbly.
Serves 6 with cornbread
*Freeze green sections of leek for soup.

YAM YUM CASSEROLE

(My way of incorporating sweet potatoes, one of my favorites, this makes a good pot luck dish.)

4 c cooked turkey, diced
3 med-size yams, peeled & quartered
1 lg apple, pared, cored, coarsely chopped
1 can condensed cream of onion soup & ½ soup can water
1 lg chicken bouillon cube
½ t ground cloves
Fresh pepper to taste

In lg oven-proof baking dish mix turkey, yams & apple.
Combine next 4 ingredients over med heat, stirring
frequently, until bouillon cube is dissolved & sauce is
blended. Pour over turkey mixture.
Bake @ 350F (180 C) for 1 hr.
Serves 6-8

BARBARA'S OVEN STEW
(Talk about "do-ahead!")

4 c cooked turkey, cubed
1 c fresh carrots, diced
1 c fresh peas (or froz)
2 onions, chopped
1 lg raw potato, peeled & sliced
1 c diced celery
1 can chicken broth
1 can condensed cream of mushroom soup
Dash Worcestershire Sauce
Parmesan cheese, grated
Salt & fresh-ground pepper to taste
Fresh mushrooms, if desired
Butter

Place layers of turkey, potatoes & vegetables in greased
casserole adding cheese and seasoning. Dot with butter
layer by layer.
Combine chicken broth & mushroom soup. Pour over
casserole, cover tightly and cook in oven @ 275F (135 C) for
5 hrs.
Serve with buttered biscuits & green salad for 4

BARBARA'S DUMPLINGS FOR STEW

(Just in case you should decide to do BARBARA'S OVEN STEW stovetop like most stews, I can't resist including Barbara's recipe for dumplings. They're not made of turkey but they certainly go well with it! You'll need to cook stew for about an hour in a covered Dutch oven or soup pot & add at least another can of broth and 1 of cream of chicken soup so that the dumplings will have something to cook on.)

1 c flour
1½ t baking powder
½ t salt
½ t sugar
2 T butter ½ c milk

Sift flour then add baking powder, salt & sugar.
Sift all together again.
Add butter by chopping into flour until it is like peas then add milk and stir until the dough is mixed.
Drop by large spoonfuls on top of stew.*
Cover and cook for 15 min.
<u>Do not lift cover or the dumplings will fall.</u>
Serves 4-6

*You can sprinkle parsley over stew just before you add the dumplings.

TOM TOM CASSEROLE

(Translation: Turkey & Tomato)

1 onion, chopped
1 clove garlic, minced
1 T olive oil
1 small can tomato paste
½ c turkey stock or chicken broth
½ c sour cream
1 T Worcestershire Sauce
2 c cooked turkey cut into ½" pieces
1 c sliced mushrooms
Salt & fresh-ground pepper to taste

In lg frying pan, sauté onion & garlic in oil.
Mix tomato paste with stock, sour cream & Worcestershire.
Stir until blended.
Add turkey & mushrooms, stirring until mixed.
Season to taste & turn into oven-proof casserole.
Bake @ 350F (180C) for 35 min.
Serve over rice for 2-3.

MY MOTHER'S TURKEY SKILLET SUPPER

2 T butter
¼ c each chopped onion & green pepper
2 c diced, cooked turkey
1 c precooked rice
1 c cream of mushroom soup
1 c water
1 t salt
¼ t tarragon
⅛ t freshly ground pepper
2 T chopped pimiento

METHOD:
1—Melt butter in skillet; sauté onion & green pepper 5 min.
2 – Add turkey & sauté another 5 min. Add rice, soup, water, salt, tarragon, pepper & pimiento.
3 – Cover & cook over low heat 10 min or until rice is tender.
Serves 4

DO-AHEAD LAYERED CASSEROLE

(The beauty in this dish lies not only in its presentation but in the fact that it can be put together early in the day or the night before and served at the last minute.)

2 (14-oz) cans diced tomatoes
1 T butter
6-oz pkg fast-cooking long grain & wild rice
3 c shredded cabbage*
3 c diced cooked turkey tossed with ½ c sour cream & 1 T flour
1 c shredded American cheese

Drain tomatoes, reserving liquid. If needed, add water to liquid to make 2½ c. Add butter with rice & seasoning packet to tomato liquid in lg heavy saucepan.
Bring to boil, cover tightly, reduce heat and cook on low until all liquid is absorbed – about 25 min.
Meanwhile, pour boiling water over cabbage. Let stand 2 min then drain and toss with flour then sour cream.
(If you have a clear 3-qt oven-proof baking dish with straight sides and deep enough to hold all this, your layered look will earn raves at serving time.)
Spoon rice into baking dish then layer cabbage mixture, turkey and reserved tomatoes.
Top with cheese and refrigerate for a couple of hours to let flavors blend while you tidy up (either your kitchen or yourself) before dinner. When you're ready, bake casserole @ 350F (180C) for 35 min.
Serves 8
*This part is even easier if you use pkgd cole slaw mix.

PINEAPPLE TURKEY AND WILD RICE

½ lb dried pineapple, cut into ½" pieces
2¼ c boiling water
1 onion, chopped
2 T butter
½ c pineapple juice
3 c diced cooked turkey
6-oz pkg fast-cooking long grain & wild rice
⅓ c coarsely chopped walnuts

Melt butter in lg covered skillet.
Pour boiling water over pineapple & let stand while sautéing onion in butter until golden.
Drain pineapple, reserving 1½ c liquid.
Add water, juice & rice to skillet. Bring to boil, cover & simmer until all liquid is absorbed – about 5 min.
Stir in turkey, pineapple & nuts.
Heat to serving temp.
Serves 6

DANNY'S MOTHER'S DIVINE LEFTOVER TURKEY

(Thank you, Amy!)

4 c cubed turkey
1 can Cream of Mushroom Soup
¾ c sliced almonds -- toasted
30-oz can of sliced mushrooms – drained
½ c (lg jar) pimiento – drained/coarse chopped
About 1 t flour to sprinkle
½ c turkey broth (¾ c if making a day ahead)
10-oz frozen peas, thawed
2-3 oz cooking Sherry
Salt & white pepper to taste
Generous celery salt, about ½ t
12-oz (3 c) grated sharp cheddar -- divided

1) Combine soup, broth & seasonings over med-hi. Sprinkle generously with flour. Heat, stirring constantly, until thick.
2) Meanwhile, combine turkey, mushrooms & pimiento in large mixing bowl.
3) When sauce is thick, remove from heat & stir in 2-oz Sherry (3-oz if making a day ahead). Pour sauce over turkey mix & gently combine.
4) When about room temperature, fold in sliced almonds, peas & ⅓ the cheese.

5) Pour into buttered 9x11 casserole. Can make ahead to this point & refrigerate overnight if desired.
6) Preheat oven to 350F (175C). Bake uncovered 20-25 minutes. Top with remaining cheese & bake 10-15 minutes more 'til bubbling, cheese melted & touched with brown.
7) Let stand 5 minutes & serve.
Serve 8-10* with French-cut green beans drizzled with lemon juice & butter, a great tossed salad – biscuits or croissants.

*If you don't want to cut this recipe in half, half of it may be frozen for another time.

SLICED TURKEY BREAST IN KATHY'S LEMON SAUCE

1) Make 1½ c white sauce.
2) Blend in 2 t chicken-seasoned stock base. (It is salty, so be careful.)
3) Squeeze in juice of ½ lemon plus a little of the rind.
4) Season with Sherry to taste.
5) Cook down until mellow.

Have ready sliced cooked turkey meat preheated to serving temperature.

Serve over 2-3 slices turkey per plate.

(Kathy tells me that sliced mushrooms are good in this sauce and must be sautéed separately. She also says that she loves this sauce over vegetables and fish.)

TURKEY-LIMA CASSEROLE

(A great way to tap into your garden when tomatoes are at their peak.)

¼ c finely chopped onion
3 T butter or 2 T olive oil
1 c Italian-seasoned canned tomatoes with juice
2 c fresh lima beans* or 1 small pkg froz, cooked
2 c cooked turkey, diced
½ c each pkgd bread crumbs & grated Parmesan cheese
Pinch each marjoram, thyme & parsley (opt)

In butter or oil, sauté onion until golden. Add tomatoes & simmer 10 min.
Precook beans.
Add limas & turkey with seasonings. Mix well. Turn into oven-proof casserole. Sprinkle with bread crumbs & cheese. Bake @ 350F (180C) 30 min until topping is browned.
Serves 3-4

*Butter beans (opt)

TURKEY FARMER'S PIE

(A beak-in-cheek takeoff on the classic Shepherd's Pie and a good use for any mashed potatoes or gravy or vegetables you may have left over from your holiday dinner.)

2 c chopped leftover turkey
2 c leftover vegetables (peas, corn, beans, carrots, etc)
1 c leftover gravy or gravy mix
2 leftover mashed potatoes

In ovenproof casserole,* combine turkey with vegetables & gravy.
Spread potatoes over top. Dot with butter & sprinkle with paprika.
Heat @ 350F (180C) for 35 min.
Serves 4

*To freeze, prepare in aluminum foil casserole. Do not heat. Cover with foil & seal in plastic bag. This tastes pretty good come mid-January or February.

TURKEY FARMERS' TWIST

For something different, if you have them, try substituting what has become that other classic, green bean/ mushroom soup/ fried onion casserole for vegetables & gravy with mashed sweet potatoes in place of white ones. Even candied sweet potatoes will work if you mash them until smooth. Dot with butter & proceed as above.

CARRY-ALONG CASSEROLE

Cook 8-oz pkg wide flat noodles.
Meanwhile, melt 2 T butter in lg skillet and blend in thoroughly 2 T flour.
Add 2 (8-oz) cans tomato sauce and simmer for 5 min.
Add 4 c cooked turkey, diced.

Blend together: 2 c cottage cheese
1 c sour cream
1 t salt
½ c chopped green onions
2 T chopped green pepper
¼ c drained & chopped ripe olives

Place half of the noodles in greased 3-qt baking dish or casserole.
Spread all of the cheese mixture over noodles.
Add remaining noodles.
Cover with turkey mixture, spreading evenly on top.
Bake uncovered @ 350F (180C) for 30 min.
Let stand about 10 min before serving at home or reheat as necessary when "carrying-along."
Serves 10-12

TURKEY MEATLOAF

(This is one of the few recipes included here which calls for uncooked ground turkey. We like it enough to share it. It's also a good time to use up any leftover mashed potatoes and gravy!)

1 lb ground turkey
½ lb each ground pork & veal
1 each lg sweet onion & red Bell pepper, chopped
1½ c cracker crumbs (You can make your own by crumbling your favorites.)
1½ c milk
2 eggs
1 T cornstarch
Salt & freshly ground pepper to taste

Combine all ingredients and pack into large loaf pan.
Bake @ 350F (180C) for one hour.

*If you're tired of mashed potatoes and gravy, try covering this with chili sauce as it bakes.

.....................TURKEY FACTS.............................

An internet search reveals only three U.S. towns and one in Canada named for the turkey.

Turkey Creek, Louisiana
Turkey, North Carolina
Turkey, Texas
Turkey Point, Ontario

All of these are said to be named for the wild turkey which inhabited the areas.

Although not indigenous to any of these places, in Arabic turkey is called "Greek chicken."

In Greek, it's known as "French chicken."

In France it's "Indian chicken."

AROUND THE WORLD IN A MEASURING CUP

BAVARIAN TURKEY WITH BEANS

(Here's another one which can come together in almost no time if you have cooked the spatzle in advance.)

2 c cooked turkey, cut in bite-size pieces
2 c cut green beans or 1 pkg froz, cooked
2 c cooked spatzle
1 can cream of mushroom soup
4 T (¼ c) milk
1 c French Fried Onions, crushed

Blend milk with soup* and toss with turkey, beans and spatzle.
Turn into oven-proof baking dish and top with onion.
Bake @ 350F (180C) for 35 min. and turn on broiler for 5 min to brown, if desired.
Serves 2-3

*Warm milk with soup to make mixing easier.

TURKEY CREOLE

1 T unsalted butter
1 T olive oil
2 c diced onion
2 c diced celery
1 c each diced red & green Bell pepper
1 clove garlic, minced
1 lg can tomatoes, crushed with juice
1 sm can tomato paste
1 c chicken broth
2 T cornstarch
¼ c Worcestershire Sauce
1 T paprika
2 t dried thyme
Salt to taste
2 c diced cooked turkey
Cooked rice

In lg heavy saucepan with cover combine butter & olive oil over med heat.
Add onion, celery Bell pepper & garlic. Sauté about 5 min.
Add tomatoes, tomato paste & broth and simmer, covered, 20 min.
Meanwhile, blend cornstarch into Worcestershire. Mix in paprika, thyme & salt and add to saucepan.
Add turkey and simmer, covered, until mixture is thickened, about 10 min.
Serve over rice.
Serves 4-6

SUMMER CHILI

(Originally featured in the June 21, 2011 issue of Woman's World Magazine *as "Money-Saving Cooking with Grandma Joan," this is one of my personal favorites. Tailored to the slow cooker, it is meant to keep your kitchen cool while low-cost beans freeze your budget!)*

Rinse <u>1 c small white beans</u> and place in slow cooker with <u>1 lb lean ground turkey.</u> (You may substitute 2 cups cooked chopped turkey.) Chop and add <u>1 large sweet onion, 1 large yellow Bell pepper, 2 medium carrots, 1 stalk celery with leaves*</u> with <u>4 cups water.</u> Add <u>2 large Knorr Chicken Bouillon Cubes</u> and <u>1 teaspoon each ground cumin, dried oregano</u> and <u>garlic salt</u> with <u>chopped jalapeño pepper to taste</u> (optional). Cover and cook on low for about 9 hours or, if you're in a hurry, on high for about 5-1/2 hours. Ladle into bowls and sprinkle with <u>shredded Parmesan cheese</u> and <u>crushed white corn chips.</u> Serves 6 and pairs well with green salad and cornbread.

*GRANDMA'S WISDOM: To save time, cut vegetables into pieces and "chop" them in your blender with as much of the water as needed.

<u>WHITE CHILI BEAN SOUP</u>
Soup lovers may want to leave vegetables in larger chunks and add 6 cups of water with 2 more bouillon cubes and a can of condensed Cream of Onion soup.

QUICK SOUTHWESTERN TURKEY STEW

4 c cooked turkey, cut into bite-sized pieces
1 onion, chopped
1 green Bell pepper, seeded & diced
1 (1 lb) can tomatoes
1 (1 lb) can red kidney beans
1 (12 oz) can kernel corn
1 t chili powder
Salt & freshly ground pepper

Drain liquid from canned vegetables into lg skillet.
Add onion & pepper. Cook until liquid is reduced to about half.
Add turkey, canned vegetables, chili powder, salt & pepper.
Heat to serving temperature.
Serve 4 with cornbread & MEXICAN BEET SALAD.

MEXICAN BEET SALAD
(If you're lucky enough to have fresh beets from your garden, you may add beet greens, washed & cut up, to this salad.)
Combine: ½ pkg mixed greens (Add those beet greens if you have them), 1 lg can Mandarin orange sections drained, 1 can beets drained (or 2 lg beets, cooked, peeled & cubed) and 4 green onions sliced. Sprinkle with olive oil, vinegar, freshly-ground garlic salt & pepper to taste.

BEV' S TURKEY ENCHILADAS

(Back when times were tough and budgets were stretched, a California neighbor shared this recipe. The kids loved it even back then when there wasn't any meat inside. We still love it and, like our budget, this recipe has improved over the years. It's a perfect place to "hide" white or dark meat from those who prefer the opposite.)

3 c cooked turkey, chopped
12 lg flour tortillas
2 cans condensed cream of chicken soup mixed with 1 soup can milk or half & half*
Salt to taste
½ lb Jack cheese or another soft mild cheese, grated

Preheat oven to 350F (180C).
Lightly grease a lg rectangular oven-proof baking dish.**
Toss turkey with small amount of soup mixture, just enough to hold mixture together.
Divide turkey mixture between tortillas.
Roll up tortillas and place in pan.
Pour remaining soup mixture over and sprinkle with cheese.
Cover with foil and bake for 45 min.
If desired, top with sliced avocado or serve with guacamole.
Serves 4

GUACAMOLE:
3 ripe avocados
2 ripe tomatoes
1 onion, chopped
About 3 T mayonnaise
1 t gr cumin
½ t garlic salt
Fresh ground pepper to taste
1 t fresh cilantro, chopped (opt)
Few drops hot sauce (opt)

Finely chop tomato & onion.
Mash with avocado & mayonnaise.
Mix in seasonings.
Chill about 1 hr then serve with tortilla chips.

*Cambell's Creamy Chicken Verde Soup is a tasty substitute.
**Non-stick cooking spray is the easy way to go. If you're
using butter or oil, you'll want to put a small plastic bag over
your hand before spreading it.

TORTILLA BEAN PIE

(Here's another one which carried us through some tough times. It's low in fat and tastes bueno!!)

1 pkg corn tortillas*
2 c cooked shredded turkey
1 can diced tomatoes & liquid mixed with 1 T gr cumin
2 cans red kidney beans**
1 lg onion, chopped
2 T chopped jalapeño pepper (opt)
1 c shredded cheddar cheese
1 small can ripe olives
Sour cream & salsa

Lightly grease bottom of round baking dish.
Begin with 2 tortillas and alternate with next 4 ingredients to make 4 layers.
Top with cheese and olives.
Bake @ 350F (180C) for 30 min.
Serve 3-4 with sour cream & salsa.

*Cut any remaining tortillas into quarters, brush with oil & bake on cookie sheet @ 350F (175c) for 10 min.
Upon removing pie from oven, stick tortilla quarters, standing up, into top of pie.
**Don't drain beans. Tortillas will absorb liquid.

MEXICAN IN MINUTES
(The secret's in the rice which goes right from box to skillet.)

2 c uncooked Minute Rice (I like the Whole Grain Brown)
2 c boiling water (Do this in microwave)
1 can condensed cream of tomato soup
1 t each dried oregano & gr cumin
1 each small can black beans & kernel corn with liquid
2 c cooked turkey, diced

In lg skillet combine rice, water, soup & seasonings. Bring to boil.
Add vegetables & turkey.
Return to boil. Cover & simmer 5 min.
Serves 4 with warm tortillas or, if you don't have time to heat them, tortilla chips & "store-bought" salad-in-a-bag with bottled dressing.

GEORGE'S ITALIAN DELIGHT
(One of my husband's boyhood favorites)

2 lg onions, chopped
½ c each green Bell pepper, celery & mushrooms (or sm can mushrooms, drained)
1 clove garlic, minced
½ c olive oil
1 can corn niblets, drained
1 lg can tomato purée
1 t chili powder
2 c diced cooked turkey
1 pkg wide flat noodles, cooked
About 1 c grated Tillamook cheese

Chop onion & pepper coarsely.
Cut celery in thin diagonal slices. Cut these in half if necessary.
Slice mushrooms.
In lg skillet sauté onion, pepper, celery, mushrooms & garlic in olive oil.
Add corn, tomato purée, chili powder, turkey & noodles.
Mix well.
Turn into oven-proof casserole.
Top with cheese.
Place casserole on baking sheet (in case of runover) in 350F (180C) oven and bake for 45-60 min.
Serves 4

TURKHETTI

(I like this better with raw ground turkey although it can be made with leftovers. Children love this and it's healthy, too!)

1½ lb ground turkey (or 3 c chopped cooked turkey)
1 lg onion, chopped
½ each yellow, red & green Bell pepper, chopped
½ pkg shredded carrots
1 small clove garlic, minced
2 T olive oil
2 cans diced tomatoes with liquid (or 4 lg tomatoes, peeled & chopped)
1 jar prepared spaghetti sauce (optional)
1 sm can tomato paste
2 T sugar
1 t dried basil
1 t dried oregano
1 t dried parsley
1 c dry white wine or chicken broth
16- oz pkg whole wheat spaghetti according to direction
Grated or shredded Italian cheese

In lg Dutch oven sauté turkey with onion, pepper, carrots and garlic until turkey looks crumbly (or add cooked turkey meat to sautéed vegetables).
Stir in next 5 ingredients and simmer sauce, stirring occasionally, for about 1½ hrs.
Serve over spaghetti & top with cheese.
Serves 8

LEFTOVER TURKEY PASTA PESTO
(Serve paired with Spinach Salad for a "company" dinner.)

2 c cooked turkey
1 sm jar prepared pesto or 1 pkg mix, prepared
1-2 c half & half
1 c grated Parmesan cheese
Sun-dried tomatoes (opt)
Cooked Angel Hair Pasta.*

While pasta cooks, place turkey with pesto & cream in lg
skillet, stirring constantly over med heat for about 2 min.
Add tomatoes if desired.
Drain pasta & toss in skillet with turkey mixture.
Sprinkle with cheese and continue to toss until well mixed.
Serves 4

*Bring lg pot of water to boil, add a splash of olive oil with a
pinch of salt (opt) and stir in raw pasta. Cover, remove from
heat and let stand 15 min. (*This is a cooking method I
learned from an Italian chef and it works for all pasta!*)

SPINACH SALAD: Toss 1 pkg baby spinach with 1 avocado,
sliced, a few raw red onion rings and a small can of
Mandarin Oranges, drained. Sprinkle with bottled Italian
Dressing.

TURKEY TETRAZZINI

(Not quite as Italian as it sounds but said to be named for a popular Italian opera singer living in San Francisco in the early 1900's. This may be divided and frozen if you don't want to cut recipe in half.)

½ pkg egg noodles, cooked
4 c leftover turkey
1 onion, chopped
12 oz mushrooms, sliced
2 T butter
1 T olive oil
1 can condensed cream of chicken soup
1 soup can stock or broth
1 soup can heavy (whipping) cream
½ c bread crumbs
1 c grated or shredded Parmesan cheese

In Dutch oven, sauté onion & mushrooms in butter & olive oil.
Blend together soup, stock & cream.
Mix with turkey & noodles.
Add to Dutch oven & moisten with more stock if necessary.
Top with bread crumbs & Parmesan.
Bake @ 350F (180C) for 35 min.
Serves 6

TURKEY DIVAN

(This is named for the New York restaurant, Divan Parisienne, responsible for the popularity of this delicious dish. It's a culinary sibling of TURKEY TETRAZZINI. This, too, freezes well should you want to divide it in half and save some for next time.)

4 c rice, cooked
4 c leftover turkey in bite-size pieces
4 c broccoli, steamed & well-drained*
2 c grated sharp white cheddar cheese

SAUCE: You can concoct a classic Mornay Sauce from scratch or you can do it my way – the *easy* way!

Combine: 1 can condensed cream of chicken soup
          ½ c heavy (whipping) cream
          ½ c stock or chicken broth
          ¼ c (4T) dry white wine or broth
          ¼ c (4T) fresh lemon juice
          2 T curry powder
          Salt & pepper to taste

In greased oven-proof dish layer as follows: rice on bottom
turkey in the middle
broccoli on top
Pour sauce over & top with grated cheese.**
Bake @ 350F (175C) for 35 min.
Serves 6

*You may use broccoli florets & reserve stalks for soup or
cut stalks into ¼" slices & include in this recipe.
**I have a friend who crumbles potato chips on the very
top.

JIFFY TURKEY CURRY WITH RAITA SALAD

(The earliest known recipe for curry is said to come from Babylon in Mesopotamia dating back to 1700 BC. Although this spicy stew-like dish is thought of as Indian, it is said that it may be the most popular restaurant item in Britain.)

1 can condensed cream of chicken soup
¼ c heavy (whipping) cream
¼ c dry white wine or chicken broth
2 T curry powder
1 T freshly ground pepper
1 T dry onion soup mix*
¼-½ t bottled browning sauce
2 c chopped cooked turkey dark meat
1 (19-oz) can diced tomato, drained
1-2 T chopped green Chile peppers
2 T fresh lemon juice
6 c cooked rice**

Assorted Condiments

In large skillet combine first 7 ingredients. Stir over med heat for 5 minutes.
Add turkey, tomato & peppers. Simmer for 2 min, stirring frequently.
Just before serving, add lemon juice.
Serve over hot rice and let diners choose condiments.

SUGGESTED CONDIMENTS:
Seedless raisins
Toasted peanuts, almonds or cashews, chopped
Chopped apple
Bottled chutney
Red currant jelly
Chopped green onion

*You may use remainder of onion soup mix with sour cream as a dip or to add flavor to turkey soup.
**You may substitute quick or ready-cooked rice.

RAITA SALAD: *(This cool, creamy salad is used to temper the heat in spicy Indian dishes.)*
Stir 2c diced cucumber & 1c chopped fresh mint into 2c plain yogurt. Add 1 t sugar, 1 t ground cumin &1 t salt. Drain in colander or strain and refrigerate 4 hrs or overnight.
Serve on bed of lettuce leaves.

EASY TURKEY SENEGALESE

(This is something different and about as simple as it gets!)

1 can condensed cream of chicken soup
¼ c (4T) heavy whipping cream
1 T curry powder
1 pkg Hollandaise Sauce Mix
6 slices cooked turkey white meat
1 green apple, finely chopped with skin on
1 c chopped peanuts

Combine first four ingredients in small saucepan over med heat.
Stir just until mixture begins to boil.
Pour over sliced turkey in oven-proof casserole.
Bake @ 350F (180C) for 15 min.
Meanwhile, prepare rice according to direction.
Serve turkey over rice and top with apple and peanuts.

ORIENTAL STIR-FRY OVER RICE

2 c raw rice
6-oz pkg froz pea pods
About 2 T peanut oil
1 c diagonally-sliced celery
½ c sliced green onion
8-oz can water chestnuts, drained & sliced
2 c cooked turkey in bite-sized pieces
¼ c Tamari
1 can chicken broth
2 T cornstarch
3 T cold water
Crisp Chinese Noodles

Cook rice & pea pods according to pkgs. Keep warm over hot water.
Meanwhile, make paste of cornstarch & water. Set aside.
Heat oil in lg skillet or wok until it begins to smoke then swirl it around to coat pan.
Over very high heat, work quickly, stirring rapidly & constantly.
Add to pan celery, green onion & water chestnuts. Cook about 5 min until celery is tender.
Add turkey & stir.
Stir in cornstarch/Tamari mixture then broth.
Cook over moderate heat, stirring until thickened.
Stir in pea pods.
Serve over rice with Chinese Noodles for garnish.
Serves 4

TURKEY-STUFFED EGGPLANT Á LA GRECQUE

(Serve with TZATZIKI, a not-so-distant cousin to the Indian RAITA listed under JIFFY TURKEY CURRY.)

2 small eggplants
1 onion, chopped
1 yellow Bell pepper, seeded & chopped
1 c cooked turkey, chopped
2 c cooked rice
1 15-19 oz can diced tomatoes with liquid
1 clove garlic, minced
1 t dried oregano
½ t ground cinnamon
½ ground cloves
1 c crumbled Feta cheese

Cut eggplants in half lengthwise.
Roast, cut-side down, in about ½" water in shallow roasting pan @ 400F (200C) for about 20 min.
Meanwhile, sauté pepper and onion in Dutch oven until onion turns golden.
Scoop out eggplant, reserving shells, chop then mix in Dutch oven with all remaining ingredients except cheese.
Cook together for 3-5 min then spoon this mixture into eggplant shells & sprinkle with Feta.
Bake 35 min @ 350F (177C).
Serves 4

TZATZIKI:
1 English cucumber, peeled & finely chopped
1½ c plain Greek yogurt
½ c sour cream
¼ c mayonnaise
1 clove garlic, minced
Salt to taste

Mash & drain cucumber in colander and press in paper towels to remove excess moisture.
You may also want to drain yogurt for an hour or so as well. Do this by placing yogurt in a fine strainer lined with cheesecloth or a paper coffee filter suspended over a funnel in lg measuring cup. Refrigerate 1 hr.
Mix all ingredients in sealable container & refrigerate 3 hrs or overnight.

MY SWEDISH MEATBALLS

(Back when — <u>way back when</u> I was learning to cook, I came across a recipe for Swedish meatballs in a magazine. It looked good, so I tried it out. It was! The original has been tweaked many times either through loss of recipe & retrieval by memory or just plain changes in taste. It remains another favorite calling for uncooked turkey but too good to overlook.)

1 lb raw ground turkey
½ lb raw ground pork
1½ c dry bread crumbs
1 lg onion, minced
1 T cornstarch
½ t dill weed
¼ t allspice
¼ t nutmeg
1 egg, whisked
1 c heavy cream or evaporated milk*
Salt & fresh ground pepper to taste
¼ c unsalted butter
½ c all-purpose flour**
1 lg chicken bouillon cube**
1 c water
1 can chicken broth
1½ t sugar
1 pkg flat noodles, cooked

Combine meat, onion & breadcrumbs with cornstarch, seasonings, egg & ½ c cream.
Mix and refrigerate 1 hr.
When well-chilled, form into meatballs.
Heat butter in lg skillet. Brown meatballs, a few at a time.
Transfer to serving platter.

SAUCE:
Mix flour & lg bouillon cube with water, stirring into smooth paste. Scrape pan & add paste.
Slowly add canned broth & remaining ½ c evaporated milk.
Cook, stirring constantly, until smooth.
Add meatballs to sauce & simmer, covered, 30 min.
Cook noodles according to pkg direction.
Serve meatballs on bed of cooked noodles garnished with sprigs of fresh dill.
Makes about 2½ doz dinner-size meatballs and 5 doz hors d'oeuvres-size.

*1 c heavy (whipping) cream has 800 calories.
  1 c evaporated milk has 320 calories.

**Dissolve flour in half of water (cold) and bouillon in other half (hot).

VI'S CANADIAN TURKEY IN CREAM WITH RICE

2-3 Slices cooked turkey
½ c sweet onion, chopped
1 c Baby Bella mushrooms, sliced
1 T unsalted butter
1 T olive oil
8 oz sour cream
2 oz dry white wine (opt)
Salt & freshly ground pepper to taste
Vi's Rice

In lg skillet sauté onion until golden.
Add mushrooms & sauté until soft.
Stir in wine, then sour cream, gradually.
Add turkey and heat to serving temp.
Serve over rice.

VI'S RICE: (Prepare ahead)
In separate covered* lg skillet place raw rice & butter.
Stir over med heat until rice begins to turn color.
Add stock or broth.
Cover & cook over very low heat about 15-18 min until
liquid is absorbed. Do <u>not</u> lift cover until rice is cooked.
Let stand, covered, 5-10 min before stirring in juice of ½
lemon to keep from sticking.
Serve turkey & cream sauce over rice.
Serves 4
*I like my glass skillet cover so that I can keep an eye on the
rice.

......................TURKEY FACTS......................

Turkeys are estimated to have 3,500 feathers at maturity.

"Big Bird" of Sesame Street fame wears a costume made of nearly 4,000 white turkey feathers dyed bright yellow!

When a bowler throws three strikes in a row, this is called "a turkey."

The Turkey Trot is a ballroom dance which takes its name from the jerky turkey.

"Turkey" is a derogatory name meaning "loser" popular in the '70's.

June is National Turkey Lovers' Month.

TAILPIECE

TABLE OF ABBREVIATIONS & EXPLANATIONS

t.......................... teaspoon

T.......................... tablespoon

lb.......................... pound

oz.......................... ounce

c.......................... cup

pt.......................... pint

qt.......................... quart

gal.......................... gallon

lg.......................... large

med.......................... medium

sm.......................... small

froz.......................... frozen

min.......................... minute(s)

ml.......................... millimeter(s)

hr.......................... hour(s)

gr.......................... ground

pkg(d).................. package(d)

opt.......................... optional

F.......................... Fahrenheit

C.......................... Centigrade

condensed...................... undiluted

cube.............................. cut into squares

dice.............................. cut into sm cubes

garnish........................... decorate

...TABLE OF ABBREVIATIONS & EXPLANATIONS

Giblets.......................... heart, liver & gizzard of fowl
glaze............................. to coat
hors doeuvres............. bits of food served as appetizers
lg bouillon cube.......... size which makes 2 c
marinade...................... oil & acid mixture such as vinegar,
                                 wine or fruit juice in which to soak
                                 food for greater flavor or tenderness
mince........................... finely chop
parboil......................... boil until partially cooked
purée........................... press through sieve or ricer or use
                                 food processor
sauté............................ cook in a little bit of fat
scant............................ about less 1 T
simmer........................ just below boiling

TABLE OF
APPROXIMATE EQUIVALENTS

60 drops....................1 t

2 t..............................1 dessert spoon

3 t..............................1 T (15 ml)

2 T.............................1 oz (30 ml)

1 oz...........................30 grams

8 oz...........................1 c (237 ml)

2 c.............................1 pt

2 pt...........................1 qt

4 qt...........................1 gal

8 qt...........................1 peck

4 peck.......................1 bushel

16 oz.........................1 lb

16 oz can..................2 c

1 lb.............................454 grams

      2 c liquid

      2 c butter

      2 c chopped or diced meat

      4 c dry cheese

      5 c freshly grated cheese

      4 c bread flour

      4½ c cake flour, sifted

      2½ c raw rice

      2 c granulated sugar

      3½ c confectioner's sugar

1 t sugar.................. ¼ grain saccharin

1 c granulated sugar.............. 1 tightly packed c brown sugar

1 c granulated sugar.............. ¾ c honey

1 lemon, juiced...................... 2-3 T

TEMPERATURE CONVERSION

Centigrade to Fahrenheit (CtoF): multiply by 9
                                  divide by 5
                                  add 32

Fahrenheit to Centigrade (FtoC): subtract 32
                                   multiply by 5
                                   divide by 9

Conversions in this book are approximate, within 5 degrees of each other.

SOURCES

American College Dictionary (Random House)
British Turkey Information Service
Canadian Encyclopedia.com
Curry – Origins and History by Cheryl Tan
Foodland Ontario
Google Turkey Trivia
Google Canada
Linda's Culinary Dictionary by Linda Stradley
     (What's Cooking America)
Mother Nature Network
National Turkey Foundation (USA)
Presidential Pardon by Borgna Brunner and Mark Hughes
Statistics Canada
University of Arkansas Division of Agriculture and
     Cooperative Extension Service

CREDITS

Cover Design: Joan Bushnell
Artist: Linda Leslie

Special thanks to Lyn Smith

WELL, HERE YOU HAVE IT. MARK MY WORD,
THE TURKEY IS AN AWESOME BIRD,
A VERSATILE AND TASTY TREAT,
IT'S PRETTY BLOOMIN' GOOD TO EAT!

--JLB

GOBBLE IT UP!

ABOUT THE AUTHOR

Joan LeGro Bushnell, a writer since the age of seven, published her first piece when she was thirteen. Primarily a playwright and songwriter (See Dramatic Publishing Company), her experience includes editing and writing for newspapers, magazines, radio, theatre and public relations. One of her favorite hobbies has made her an accomplished cook.

NOTES.............

CPSIA information can be obtained
at www.ICGtesting.com
Printed in the USA
FFOW03n1403160913
1783FF